THE BO CAGE: A STORY IN LETTERS & FRAGMENTS

~

KRISTINA MARIE DARLING

GOLD Wake Press

Boston, Ma

THE BODY IS A LITTLE GILDED CAGE: A STORY IN LETTERS & FRAGMENTS

TABLE OF CONTENTS

~

"I go where I love and where I am loved, into the snow...."
—H.D., *Trilogy*

~

CITY WALK

When our taxi arrives, I brush the soot from my long white sleeves. Your gold cigarette case flips open & I begin to notice the stains on your French silk cuff. My eyes affixed to its luminous glass button. Now the windows darken one by one & from the sidewalk, every back light seems to smolder. We fasten each latch on the car's metal door & I watch, exultant, as your cigarette burns & burns—

SOIRÉE

When we arrive at the party, a woman spills wine on your black suede shoes. The lilies are blooming & tonight, she aches with melancholia in her dark green dress. Beneath its rhinestone clasp a tinderbox & you are the restless spark. Soon you're smoldering as the phonograph turns & turns. Its song unravels like my bright yellow corsage & now both of you are humming along—

Soirée (ii)

As the dance hall murmurs, I'm having a dream of you. My telephone stifles your voice like the vases clutch their exotic red lilies, so I send a wire off. The paper unfurls & you see that the word "fire" is not "fin de siècle." Soon I'm knocking at your window & a strange woman says you've gone back to the party. All night the sky towers above us like a cathedral & you are indifferent as a dusty marble saint—

CITY WALK (II)

We take a walk through the city to observe its
rituals, their intricate structure. The cathedral
heaves with its nightly choral exultation & I begin to
imagine us kneeling beneath the towering white
arcades. Our eyes adrift along their beveled iron
trim. Now the windows darken & every statue
seems to shudder. Your hymnal flies open & I see
that its psalms are written in a dead language—

CITY WALK (III)

Your letter arrives & I take a walk through Vienna
in my pale blue dress. The chapel groans with its
nightly organ recital & I remember us listening
among the rows of wooden pews. A chorus rising as
you counted the buttons on my stiff white sleeves.
Now the city darkens with nostalgia & every
streetlamp seems to smolder. Your green shutters
fly open & still the problem of expressing these
things—

Soirée (iii)

The music begins & we watch dancers stumble beneath dim chandeliers. Their faces blur in every mirror & I imagine us adrift among the hall's towering white pillars. My heart a room opening inside a darkened room. Now each balustrade glitters with empty crystal & the guests can only murmur. The phonograph keeps turning & soon the night is a pearl necklace I've locked away with a silver key—

AVIARY

A cold moon rises over glittering cages & you fasten the lock on each silver door. The sparrows are nesting & I begin to count the buttons on your black wool coat. My eyes adrift along its luminous satin inlay. Now the night has been opened like a box of exotic blue canaries & I'm brushing feathers from my long dark sleeves. You smile as the song rises, hesitant, in my cool white throat—

APPENDIX A:
NOTES & OTHER MISC.

Notes to a History of Bird Keeping

Alone in the attic, she could hear his pigeons moaning in the eaves. Their dirty feathers drifting along the ledge.

✿

His presentation of the booklet, with its fragile map and array of folded lists, instilled in her a sense of stewardship. The dried violets crumbling from its endless white pages.

✿

She began to notice inconsistencies in the book's diagrams. Each feather was still displayed in its proper season. In every bone, a small memento.

✿

Thus the pursuit of anatomy revealed itself as a topography of his imagination. Its mountainous vistas and expansive polar region.

✿

Now the book as field guide. As hieroglyphic
inscription.

✿

Within the narrative, a pigeon warbling to the lost
Mussorgsky suite. Its ostentatious throat and
colorless eyes.

✿

It was then she considered the author of the
ornithological treatise. His pale hands and perfectly
groomed fingernails.

✿

Her name inscribed in the work's lengthy index.
Only when she turned the page would the violets
come into bloom.

Footnotes to a History of the Corsage

_____

[1.] Two of the darkest lilies, which he fastened at the
shoulder of her green silk dress.

[2.] On nights like this the dance hall groaned with
their erratic foxtrot. A phonograph spinning
beneath dim chandeliers.

[3.] "I had wanted to transcend the ordinary, with its
brick houses and gardens of white crocuses. Now
the most bourgeois ribbons gathered at my wrist."

[4.] *Courtship.*

    1. The act, period, or art of seeking   love
with the intent to marry.

        †2. A set of inherited conventions or
customs.

        ‡3. The solicitation of praise, favors, etc.

[5.] The mural depicts her attempt to maintain a noctuary, detailing his adulation of her finer points. Despite numerous scholarly articles devoted to the work's inscription, art historians have not yet discovered the fate of her milky-eyed beloved.

[6.] She slipped a flower in his coat pocket to preserve the ritual, its delicate structure. But before long the music stopped. The phonograph still spinning beneath its luminous needle.

[7.] The film (c. 1933) follows a woman through a series of broken engagements. Although several attempts have been made to differentiate between the four men, the problem seems intrinsic to her own psychology.

8. *Melancholia*. A state of mourning for the lost object.

9. "It was then I remembered the dance hall, his ominous presentation of the corsage. A manicured garden held by the most intricate clasp."

10. When she unpinned the lilies, a quiet upheaval. The most startling numbness in each of her fingertips.

FOOTNOTES TO A HISTORY OF PSYCHOANALYSIS

---

[1] A lengthy message, in which she describes the analyst's shelves of priceless Egyptian statuettes.

[2] In order to effectively describe the recurring dream, in which a luminous white horse appeared to her, she sent a wire after their office had closed. The steel dials clicking into the dark blue night.

[3] "Ever since I had wished for the collection, but also the role of its proprietor. To catalogue his little Vishnu idols and the disquieting canopic jars."

[4.] *Disturbance.*

    1. A distressed mental state.

    †2. An interruption or intrusion.

    3. A minor movement of the earth, often resulting in a small earthquake or the formation of a mountain.

[5.] According to Havelock Ellis, author of *The World of Dreams* (1911), her luxurious chalet alone did not constitute a refuge. It was only after the blizzard, when the region's telegraph wires had collapsed under ice, that she could be said to have retreated from the conflict.

6. Every house in the province contained an elaborate display of bone china, which was rimmed with tiny black crocuses. Before long she found herself enthralled by the luxurious dishes. Her notebooks compare their dark flowers to a silhouette projected against towering snowdrifts.

7. The album depicts his collection of Mediterranean sea glass and various relics from the shrines of saints. While several attempts have been made to recover the artifact, it is suspected to have been lost in the avalanche.

8. *Vorstellen*. Translated from the German as *imagined*.

9. To reconcile the disparity between her mind and the external world, the analyst prompted her to maintain a record of these perceptions.

10. Upon examination, her small red notebook contained the most elaborate diagrams. Even the mountainous vistas were depicted as intricate machines.

11. The message sent after their final session, in which she describes his prized statue shattered on the ledge.

FOOTNOTES TO A HISTORY OF THE CATHEDRAL

[1.] A series of tiny wooden doors, which lead only to empty rooms.

[2.] She fastened the locks as the choir began to sing. The corridor groaning with her uneven footsteps.

[3.] Meaning the lace on her skirt, which became ensnared in the ruined glass. These windows, which depicted the miracles of St. Sebastian, were ruptured by excessive smoke in the first of the great fires.

4. "I had wanted to discover the inner workings of this luminous machine. Now the most sacred relic shattered at my feet."

5. *Enshrine.*

>   1. To cherish as holy or sacred.
>   †2. To express adoration by enclosing the beloved object.

6. An early nineteenth century novel, in which the heroine believes her dead lover to be trapped inside the arcades of a cathedral. This recurring motif extends well into the novel's lengthy appendix and its maps of the hidden rooms.

7. "I began to doubt his claim that divine providence extends below the sun and moon. And now the darkest glass towering above every marble statue."

8. *Voy au malheur*. Translated from the French as *fated*.

9. A little-known film, in which the heroine lights candles for each of the soldiers who were lost in the Great War. Although never found, her fiancé could be heard singing from the cathedral's vaulted iron ceiling.

[10.] She remembered only the martyr in the stained-glass window. The silver arrows poised to kill.

[11.] The endless shards of colored glass. Every stone burned to the ground.

Footnotes to a History of the Chandelier

[1.] Each candle was affixed to an iron stake, which rose from the chandelier's intricately welded crown.

[2.] She lit the wicks when the shades were drawn. Their light stuttering into the hall's beveled mirrors.

[3.] "Even my dreams unfurled in the most Neoclassical style. Within each room, a gilt cornice framing the portentous chandelier. In every champagne glass the most brutal display of light."

4. *Luminous.*
    †1. Radiating or reflecting illumination.
    2. Intellectually revelatory or enlightening.
    3. The quality of being intelligible.

5. A lost chapter of the manuscript, in which she realizes the otherworldly nature of her beloved. This intricate Faustian motif extends well into the novel's *denouement* and its prose diagrams of the evil city.

6. Every house in the province contained a hidden staircase, which was lit by the most exotic chandelier. At night she would lie on her back and count the endless tiers of Bohemian crystal. The ominous smoldering of the candles.

7. *Malcontreuse*. Translated from the French as *star-crossed*.

8. After the fire, she remembered the dance hall. Its beveled mirror and perfect rows of white tables.

9. "I had wanted to preserve the strange white light that shone that evening. Now the most barren ashes scattered on the lawn."

10. Meaning, in this case, to discover or unearth.

11. An early *bildungsroman*, in which the heroine retained an unusual fascination with fire. Her coming of age involved a cremation of childhood mementos. For a more detailed list, see Appendix B.

FOOTNOTES TO A HISTORY OF THE PHONOGRAPH

[1.] An early version of the device, which registered sound as a furrow in an otherwise pristine metal surface.

[2.] When she cranked its little handle, the room seemed to darken.   From the ivory horn a contralto warbled the lost Puccini overture. Her flawless pitch and overwrought vibrato.

[3.] "It was only then I began to document the oddities of this strange machine. Its needle glistening as the cylinder turned and turned."

[4.] *Record.*

> 1. To set down in writing for the purpose of preserving evidence.
> †2. The tracing, marking, or the like, made by a recording instrument.
> ‡3. Something or someone serving as a remembrance.

[5.] A discarded chapter of her manuscript, in which she believed her phonograph to be haunted by a Danish psychoanalyst. This intricate gothic motif extends well into the novel's final chapter and its lengthy description of her mountainside chalet.

[6.] *Voix du passé.* Translated from the French as "voice of the past."

[7.] Because of the constant emanation of forgotten arias from her window, residents of the city believed her to be an intense, if not insatiable, audiophile.

8. "I had wanted to understand the most intricate workings of the machine. Its silver gears lay dismantled and still the most brutal onslaught of sound."

9. An untitled painting, which renders her Swish chalet as a staircase leading into the wilderness.

10. The next morning, they found sheet music rustling beneath the white piano. An empty space where the apparatus had been.

A History of the Phonograph: Glossary of Terms

benzine. Part of an early system of recording, which made use of beeswax and ether. When sounds were reproduced—at a garden party, for example—the device's radium dials could be seen shimmering beneath her mother's beveled mirror.

beeswax. A template onto which the music was inscribed. When still fairly untested, she feared that it would cleave beneath the weight of Rachmaninoff's magnum opus as it unfurled like an exotic red lily.

emboss. To impress upon, usually with the intent of preserving. Between movements the phonograph seemed to turn more slowly, heavy with the wilted corsages of last season.

phonautograph. A precursor to the garden party. The lilies she had unpinned from her green silk dress.

record. A series of etchings from which sounds are replayed. Once her memory was shown to be unreliable, numerous attempts were made at translating these intricate hieroglyphs.

spiral. Considered the *raison d'etre* of the recording's fidelity. For a more extensive documentation, see Appendix C.

stylus. A tool most often used for embossing. Throughout Europe, the leading debutantes had professed a fascination with subjectivity, and so this instrument fell out of fashion.

Notes on the Fin de Siècle

He mentions only the opulent red lace on her garter, forgetting its cluster of violet ribbons. Their intricate knots unraveling as she ascended the tiny staircase.

✿

She remembers that year for its lengthy periods of mourning. Her elaborate displays of miniature portraits and lifeless clocks.

✿

Thus his presentation of the bracelet, with its dark green ornaments and lock of tangled hair, seemed unusual, even mythical.

✿

Now the century as gilded. As a field of blue lilies.

✿

She kept the bracelet in a locked drawer to preserve its luster. The silver chain tarnishing on a red velvet pillow.

✿

The violet ribbon on her garter was dyed black at
the end of the season. Only then did she consider
the gradual change in her attire. Its darkening lace
and starched taffeta sleeves.

✿

In the winter months, lilies continue to bloom under
glass. Her insatiable interest in hermetic methods of
preservation.

APPENDIX B:
CORRESPONDENCE

Dearest   ,

       you were like

bits of broken glass-pictures in a cathedral

             night & some Greek island

       this is not much of a letter

Dearest   ,

one never hears anything from you &

think of it as fragility

I'll do anything

Dearest   ,

       that night with your silver cufflinks

            & darkened windows

       a corsage wouldn't have lasted

Dearest   ,

      in the dance hall

with its noise & shattered glass

            one would have never known

      you were like an exotic red lily

Dearest   ,

      it was birds, birds, music, the sea

          & also a dream within a dream

      I woke to burnt candles

Dearest   ,

there was only a dark pigeon, a dove

& a cold white moon

all we can do now is look backward

Dearest   ,

you are such a reticent bird

Dearest   ,

       I haven't forgotten your beating heart

                & brittle hair

       you shouldn't expect to see me again

Appendix C:
Posthumous Fragments

✿

at the party

she aches

& you

unravel

✿

a dream of

red lilies,

the word "fire"

& all night the sky

✿

the cathedral

    & each of its psalms

✿

your letter arrives,

    a chorus rising

as the city darkens

❁

my heart

locked away

with a silver key

✿

       I begin to

smolder
      & burn

✿

night

& a song

in my white throat

NOTES

The prose poems in the first section of the book, as well as the section entitled "Correspondence," take liberties with H.D.'s letters to Richard Aldington, as well as the letters sent during her psychoanalysis with Sigmund Freud.

The poem sequence "City Walk" owes a title debt to Kathleen Rooney and Elisa Gabbert.

ACKNOWLEDGEMENTS

Thank you to the editors of the following journals, in which early versions of these poems first appeared:

elimae

Gargoyle

SOFTBLOW

Spork Press

Third Coast

Word For/Word

Additional thanks to the Vermont Studio Center for the generous gift of time and feedback. Last but not least, I'm grateful to the Elizabeth George Foundation for providing wings of flight.

Kristina Marie Darling is the author of two full-length poetry collections: *Night Songs* (Gold Wake Press, 2010) and *Compendium* (Cow Heavy Books, 2011). She has been awarded fellowships from Yaddo, the Ragdale Foundation, and the Virginia Center for the Creative Arts, as well as grants from the Vermont Studio Center and the Elizabeth George Foundation. Her editorial projects include an anthology, *narrative (dis)continuities: prose experiments by younger american writers* (VOX Press, 2011), and a volume of critical essays forthcoming from Cambridge Scholars Press.

CPSIA information can be obtained at www.ICGtesting.com
Printed in the USA
BVOW04s1845220913

331848BV00002B/50/P